LONG JUMP

by Bruce Longden

(National Athletics Coach)

First Edition (D. C. V. Watts)	1949
Second Impression	1952
Third Impression	1957
Fourth Impression	1963
Second Edition (D. C. V. Watts)	1968
Third Edition (D. Kay)	1976
Fourth Edition (M. Arnold)	1987
This Edition	1995

ISBN 0 85134 127 6   2.5K/49.5K/03.95

© BRITISH ATHLETIC FEDERATION
225A Bristol Road
Birmingham B5 7UB

Typeset in Times, designed, printed on 115gsm
Fineblade Cartridge and bound by
Woodcote Ltd., Epsom, Surrey KT18 7HL, England

About the Author

Bruce Longden has been a National Coach since 1977. Firstly he was based in the South of the Thames region (1977-1984), during which period he was National Chief Coach for Jumps and Combined Events. From 1984-1988 he was Chief Coach in Norway where his special event responsibilities were the Jumps, Hurdles and Combined Events. On returning to National Coaching in Great Britain in 1990 he was appointed Chief Coach responsible for Hurdles and Combined Events, whilst having regional responsibility for the North of the Thames region of the South of England. In 1994 he was given special event responsibility for 400m Hurdles.

Contents

Acknowledgements

To my wife, Julie, for all her hard work and imaginative interpretation of my writing from the scripts.

To all my colleagues, past and present, whose material has provided much of the information in this rewrite.

To Julie Hollman and Noel Levy who managed to keep a straight face for the photographs.

Photographs

The cover photo of Heike Drechsler (Germany), Olympic and World Champion, is by Mike Hewitt /Allsport. The photosequence of her is by Helmar Hommel, and that of Larry Myricks (USA) is by the late Dr. Howard Payne. The photo of Mark Forsyth is by Gray Mortimore/Allsport. All other photographs are by Bruce Longden.

Introduction

On being requested to make the revision of this BAF coaching booklet, I must admit to being slightly bemused. There are many experts out in the field who could perhaps have done more credit to this first class series of instructional books.

However, on further thought, much of my long jump coaching has been carried out with all-rounders, the combined events athletes. Further to what has already been said in previous editions of this book, it becomes evermore obvious that the message we try to put over in many of our technical events is that we need fit, fast, multi-talented athletes who have a broad base of ability. This applies particularly to long jump. Onto this base these athletes will be able to build an explosive technique and move the event on from the halcyon days of the 1960s. That was a long time ago, but Lynn Davies still has a hold over our long jumpers 30 years on. and Mary Rand's best jump has only been exceeded by three British women.

Why is this? Perhaps we try to leap before we can run. Do we do the basics correctly? Do we expect athletes to move on automatically when perhaps more groundwork is required? What I have done in this revision is attempt to provide additional coaching points to those already made by my illustrious colleagues. They have already given a wealth of information, much of which I have maintained because it is very relevant, and still holds its value today.

I hope we have some persistent coaches out there who will find some value in what follows, and will allow Lynn Davies the pleasure of being a former record holder.

CHAPTER ONE
The History of Long Jumping

Jumping is a very natural human activity and the keen observer will notice that children enjoy all types of games involving jumping. It is this natural aspect that teachers and coaches should seize upon in the early stages of instruction. The principles of take off and landing can easily be instituted in conjunction with the many jumping games that children play, and in the gymnasium during movement education lessons.

The origins of formalised long jumping in organised competitions can be traced back to Neolithic cave drawings, showing men jumping over animals. The mythology of almost every people tells of stories of great jumping feats. Phaylus, a Greek jumper, was reputed to have jumped 55 feet, but this must have been a multiple jump of some description.

The long jump was included in the Olympic Games of the Ancient Greek world. Norman Gardner, in "Athletics of the Ancient World", provides us with a very accurate description of their methods.

"For the long jump a firm hard take off was provided, called the threshold. We do not know if it was of wood or stone. In vase paintings the take off is marked by spears stuck in the ground, or by stone pillars similar to those used to mark the start of a race. The ground in front of the take off was dug up and levelled to a certain distance. This was called the skamma. To 'jump beyond the skamma' was the expression for an extraordinary feat – Phaylus, the hero of that fabulous jump of 55 feet, is said to have jumped 5 feet beyond the skamma and we are not surprised to hear from one commentator that he broke his leg in the performance . . ."

The Greeks always used jumping weights, halteres, in the long jump. These weights, which somewhat resembled and were possibly the origin of dumbells, were made of metal or stone and varied from 2 pounds to more than 10 pounds in weight. The jumper with weights depends for his impetus partly on the swing of these weights, partly on the run. The run is short and not fast. As the jumper takes off he swings the weight forward, so that in mid-air arms and legs are almost parallel. Before landing he swings them backwards, a movement which shoots the legs to the front and so lengthens the jump.

Jumpers in Britain in the last century used jumping weights to increase their natural jumping distance. By using them, a jumper could unnaturally affect the flight path of his centre of gravity and thus gain further distance. English professional jumpers of the 19th century used all sorts of tricks, from using jumping weights to elevated take off ramps. One story tells us that "J. Howard jumped 29ft 7in (9.02 metres) at Chester in 1854". It was stated that the use of weights "added at least 8 feet to his jump". No doubt an elevated take off ramp added a little more also!

In the modern Olympic Games long jump for men was in the programme from the first games in Athens in 1896, but the women's event was not included until 1948. British success in this event has been limited. An Irishman, Pat Leahy, won a bronze medal in Paris in 1900 and Lynn Davies won on a memorable occasion in Tokyo in 1964. Shirley Cawley won her bronze in Helsinki in 1952. Mary Rand made 1964 a really memorable "long jump" Games for Britain by also winning in Tokyo with a new world record. Sheila Sherwood won a silver in Mexico City in 1968. The British medal tally has not been added to since Sue Telfer (née Hearnshaw) won a bronze medal in Los Angeles in 1984.

The Olympic Games has a long history of notable performances in long jump, not the least being the fact that the American men have won 19 of the 21 competitions they have contested (the USA did not send a team to Mexico in 1980), with only William Pettersson of Sweden (1920) and Lynn Davies (1964) interrupting the sequence of the great Americans. Very notable was Jesse Owens winning the gold medal in the 1936 Olympics, having previously set a world record of 8.13m in Ann Arbor, Michigan in 1935. That world record lasted for 25 years, until another American Ralph Boston jumped 8.21m in 1960. The Olympic Games of 1968 were held at altitude in Mexico City (7,500ft approx) with less air resistance and less gravitational problems. Bob Beamon took the opportunity to put the record on ice for a number of years (23) with his first jump which exceeded both 28 feet and 29 feet. His jump of 29ft 2½in (8.90m), done in the first round, basically 'killed' the competition. This Olympic record still stands today, though the feat of Carl Lewis in winning the Olympic long jump in both 1988 and 1992 must rank highly in Olympic history.

The world record established by Beamon withstood all until 1991 when Mike Powell broke it during the World Championships in Tokyo with 8.95m. This was followed closely in the same competition by Carl Lewis with the third best ever performance of 8.87m. These two men, plus another American Larry Myricks, hold 28 of the top 30 performances of all time. The only man apart from Beamon to break into this domination was Robert Emmiyan (USSR), with an 8.86m altitude performance in 1987.

Women's long jumping has also had a series of dominating athletes in recent years. However the first 6m jump was recorded by Christel Schulz (Germany) in 1939. This record was improved upon by Fanny Blankers-Koen who jumped 6.25m, figures which stood for 11 years (1943-54). The record then progressed towards 7m gradually through to 1978, when the first 7m plus jump was made. This breakthrough was made by Vilma Bardauskiene (USSR). It started a minor explosion of 7m plus jumps leading to one of 7.27m by Anisoara Cusmir (Romania), who took the record on to 7.43m in 1983. In 1986 it was broken by Heike Drechsler (Germany) with two jumps of 7.45m, equalled by Jackie Joyner-Kersee in 1987. Then in 1988 Galina Chistyakova (USSR) jumped 7.52m. Whilst Heike Drechsler has improved her 7.45m on to 7.48m, the world record still stands at 7.52m. The performance of Drechsler at altitude of 7.63m was unfortunately also a windy performance.

The British record for women held by Mary Rand from 1959 to 1983, was broken by Beverley Kinch with a jump of 6.90m which still stands today.

Some Landmarks in Long Jumping

Men
1874 First Briton, John Lane, jumps over 7 metres
1900 First Briton, Peter O'Connor, jumps over 7.50 metres
1901 Peter O'Connor is credited with the first World Record of 7.61 metres
1935 Jesse Owens becomes the first athlete to jump 8 metres
1964 First Briton, Lynn Davies, jumps over 8 metres
1964 Lynn Davies becomes the first British Olympic long jump champion
1968 Lynn Davies sets the present British record 8.23 metres
1968 Bob Beamon becomes the first athlete to jump over 28 feet, 29 feet and 8.50 metres and sets a World and Olympic record, all with the same winning jump of 8.90 metres at the Olympic Games in Mexico City
1991 Mike Powell wins the World Championships in Tokyo with a World Record of 8.95 metres, followed in second place by Carl Lewis with 8.87 metres '

1992 Carl Lewis retains his long jump Olympic Games title in Barcelona with 8.67 metres, having qualified for the final with 8.68 metres.

Women
1928 Kinoue Hitomi becomes the first recognised holder of the World Record at 5.98 metres, which she holds for 11 years
1939 Christel Schulz becomes the first athlete to jump over 6 metres
1952 Shirley Cawley wins a bronze medal in the Olympic Games in Helsinki
1954 Jean Desforges becomes the first Briton to jump over 6 metres
1962 Tatyana Schelkanova becomes the first athlete to jump over 6.50 metres
1964 Mary Rand becomes the first Briton to jump over 6.50 metres
1964 Mary Rand wins an Olympic gold medal in Tokyo and sets the world record at 6.76 metres

1968 Sheila Sherwood wins a silver medal in the Olympic Games in Mexico City
1978 Vilma Bardauskiene becomes the first to jump over 7 metres
1983 Beverley Kinch sets the present British record at 6.90 metres in the first World Championships in Helsinki
1984 Sue Telfer wins an Olympic bronze medal in the Olympic Games in Los Angeles
1986 Heike Drechsler sets the World Record of 7.45 metres on two occasions
1987 Jackie Joyner-Kersee jumps 7.45 metres
1988 Galina Chistyakova establishes the present world record of 7.52 metres
1992 Heike Drechsler jumps 7.48 metres and also 7.63 metres (windy +2.1 and also at altitude).

Lists of Record holders, both World and British, can be found at the end of this book.

ATHLETICS COACH
The Coaching Bulletin of the B.A.F.

Published
March, June, September, December

Details from
B.A.F. Coaching Office
225A Bristol Road, Birmingham B5 7UB

CHAPTER TWO

The Rules of Long Jumping

The following extracts are reprinted from BAF rules for competition (1994/95 edition).

COMPETITION RULES – FIELD EVENTS

120

(1) A draw shall be made to decide the order in which competitors shall take their trials and this order should be printed in the programme. The judges shall have the power to alter this order. Competitors cannot hold over any of their trials to a subsequent round.

(2) If competitors are entered in both a track event and a field event or in more than one field event taking place simultaneously, the judges may allow them to take their trials in an order different from that decided upon prior to the start of the competition.

(3) In throwing and jumping for distance no competitor is allowed to have more than one trial recorded in any one round of the competition.

(4) Competitors who unreasonably delay making a trial in a field event render themselves liable to having the trial disallowed and recorded as a fault, and for a second delay at any time during the competition to disqualification from taking any further trials, but any performances previous to the disqualification shall stand for inclusion in the final result of the competition.

(5) It is a matter for the Referee to decide, having regard to all the circumstances, what is an unreasonable delay. The following time should not normally be exceeded-

(a) in HJ, LJ, TJ - one and a half minutes (90 secs)

(c) the period between two consecutive trials by the same athlete should never be less than 3 minutes.
Note: If the time allowed elapses once the competitor has started a trial, that trial should not for that reason be disallowed.

(6) If in the opinion of the Referee the conditions warrant it, that official shall have power to change the place of the competition in any field event. Such a change should be made only after a round is completed.

(7) If for any reason a competitor is hampered in a trial in a field event the Referee shall have power to award a substitute trial.

(8) Where in any of the field events the organisers or the Referee consider it advantageous a qualifying round shall be held prior to the competition proper.

(a) All competitors who reach the prescribed standard in the qualifying round or pool shall compete in the competition proper. If less than the prescribed number of competitors reach the qualifying standard, then the leading athletes up to the prescribed number shall take part in the competition proper; where necessary Rules 121(7), 126(3) or 130(3) shall be used to decide the qualifiers. If a tie for the final place in the competition remains after these Rules have been applied, all those competitors so tying shall be included in the competition proper.

(b) In each qualifying round each competitor shall be allowed three trials, but the performance accomplished shall not be considered part of the competition proper. Once competitors have reached the qualifying standard they shall not take any more trials.

(9) If qualifying rounds or pools are held the order for taking trials in the competition proper shall be determined by a fresh draw.

When in accordance with the Rules the best competitors are allowed three more trials, they shall take their trials in the same order as laid down for the first three rounds.

(10) In any athletics meeting competitors shall be excluded from participating in further events, including Relays, when they have qualified in preliminary rounds/or pools/or heats for further participation in any event but then do not compete further without giving a valid reason to the Referee. If the meeting extends over more than one day the exclusion shall apply to all subsequent events of the meeting.

Note: This is not to be read as infringing the rights of competitors qualified under Rules 126(1)(b) or 130(1)(b) from opting out of one or more of their additional trials since they are already qualified for inclusion in the final result.

(11) Once a competition has begun competitors are not permitted to use runways or take off areas for practice or warm up purposes.

Specific Horizontal Jumps Rules

Rule 126 – General Conditions

(1) The competition may be decided in either of the following ways:

(a) Each competitor being allowed from three to six trials; or

(b) Each competitor being allowed three trials and the eight best being allowed three more trials (see Rule 120(9)). In the event of a tie for the final place(s), any competitor so tying shall be allowed the three additional trials.

(Tying means, in this connection, achieving the same distance and Rule 126(3) should not, therefore, be applied.)

To qualify for these further trials the athlete must have achieved a valid performance. The competition conditions must be explained to the competitors before the event begins.

(2) Competitors shall be credited with the best of all their trials, including jumps taken in resolving a first place tie.

(3) In the case of a tie, the second best performance of the competitors tying shall determine the result. If the tie remains, the third best jump will be decisive and so on. If the tie still remains and it concerns first place, the competitors so tying shall have such additional extra trials as are required to determine the tie. If the tie concerns any other place, the competitors shall be awarded the same place in the competition.

(4) The take-off shall be from a board the edge of which nearer to the landing area-shall be called the 'take-off line'. If a competitor takes off before reaching the board, it shall not for that reason be counted as a failure.

(5) The distance of the run is unlimited.

(6) No marks shall be placed on the runway, but a competitor may place marks alongside the runway. No competitor may place, or cause to be placed, any mark beyond the 'take-off line'.

(7) It shall be counted as a failure if any competitor:

(a) touches the ground beyond the take-off line or take-off line extended with any part of the body, whether running up without jumping or in the act of jumping.

(b) takes off from outside either end of the board, whether beyond or behind the take-off line extended.

(c) in the course of landing, touches the ground outside the landing area nearer to the take-off line than the break in the sand to which the measurement of the jump would have been made.

(d) before leaving the landing area after a completed jump, walks back through the landing area.

(e) employs any form of somersaulting.

(8) The measurement of the jump shall be made at right angles from the nearest break in the ground in the landing area made by any part of the body of the competitor to the take-off line. Only valid trials shall be measured.

(9) The distance shall be recorded to the nearest 1cm below the distance measured if that distance is not a whole centimetre.

(10) If calibrated measuring equipment is used its accuracy must be checked with a steel tape; otherwise a steel tape should be used and the part of the tape showing the distance jumped must be held at the take-off line. Alternatively a scientific apparatus, which has a certificate of accuracy from a nationally recognised standardising organisation may be used.

(11) Whenever possible wind velocity should be measured and recorded.

(a) The gauge should be set up at 20m from the take-off line, not more than 2m from, and parallel to the edge of the runway

and at a height of approximately 1.22m.

(b) The velocity shall be measured for a period of 5 seconds from the time a competitor passes a mark placed 40m (Long Jump) or 35m (Triple Jump) from the take-off line. If a competitor runs less than 40m or 35m as the case may be, the reading shall be taken from the time the athlete commences the run.

(c) The wind gauge shall be read in metres per second, rounded to the next higher tenth of a metre per second in the positive direction. (For example, a reading of +2.03m/sec. shall be recorded as +2.1m/sec; a reading of -2.03m/sec shall be recorded as -2.0m/sec). (See also Rule 141(14) and (19).

Rule 127 - General Specifications

(1) A take-off board shall be rigidly fixed in the ground, flush therewith. It shall be made of wood 1.21-1.23m long, 19.8-20.2cm wide and maximum 10cm deep, and painted white.

(2) The runway should be level. The length of the runway is unlimited but its minimum length shall be 40m but 45m is desirable if conditions permit.

(3) The minimum width of the runway shall be 1.22m.

(4) For record purposes the maximum allowance for lateral inclination of the runway must not exceed 1:100 and in the running direction 1:1000 downwards.

(5) In order that jumps can be measured accurately the sand in the landing area should be moistened before the competition.

(6) The surface of the sand in the landing area should be level with the top of the take-off board.

(7) Immediately beyond the take-off line there shall be placed a rigid board of plasticine or other suitable material for recording the athlete's footprint in the case of a foot fault. The specifications for the plasticine indicator board are as follows:

(a) The board shall be rigid, 93-102mm wide and 1.21- 1.22m long. At least the 14mm closest to the take-off board shall be covered with plasticine or other suitable material on the top surface.

(b) The surface shall rise from the level of the take-off board at an angle of 30° in the direction of running to a maximum height above the take-off board of 7mm.

(c) The board shall be mounted in a recess or shelf in the runway, on the side of the take-off board nearer the landing area. When mounted in this recess, the whole assembly must be sufficiently rigid to accept the full force of the athlete's foot.

(d) The surface of the board beneath the plasticine shall be of a material in which the spikes of an athlete's shoe will grip and not skid.

Note: The layer of plasticine can be smoothed off by means of a roller or suitably shaped scraper for the purposes of removing the footprints of the competitors,

(8) If it is not possible to install an Indicator Board as specified in (7), soft earth or damp sand should be sprinkled to a height of 7mm above the level of the take-off board over a width of 10cm beyond the edge of the board nearer to the landing area. At the take-off line the sand should be raised at an angle of 30° to the height of 7mm.

(9) The landing area should have a minimum width of 2.75m, a maximum width of 3m, and should be at least 9m long. It should, if possible, be so placed that the middle of the runway, if extended, would coincide with the middle of the landing area.

Note: When the axis of the runway is not in line with the centre of the landing area this shall be achieved by placing a tape which shall delimit a landing area which has the same width on either side of the central axis of the runway prolonged.

Figure 1

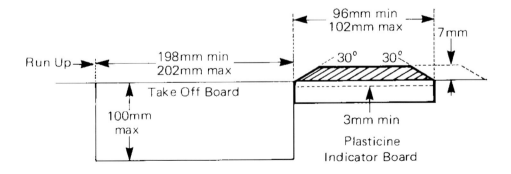

Figure 2 – **Centralised Long Jump/Triple Jump Landing Area**

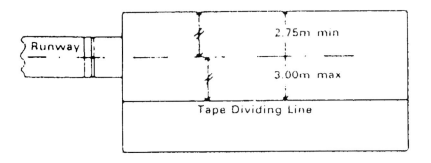

Rule 128 - Long Jump

(1) Rules 120, 126 and 127 apply.

(2) A space of at least 1m but no more than 3m, of a similar surface to the runway, should be left between the take-off board and the landing area.

(3) The distance between the take-off board and the end of the landing area should be at least 10m.

CHAPTER THREE

The Basics We Need to Know (Biomechanical Fundamentals)

What makes successful jumpers at whatever level they are competing? Perhaps we can agree that speed, spring and a special technical awareness, which varies from athlete to athlete, are the core elements of a potential 'long' jumper. The athlete who can control the highest horizontal velocity (speed) and is able to convert that speed at take off with a high vertical velocity of the centre of gravity, should in most cases jump the furthest.

We are, however, aware that it is not as simple as that, because it is impossible to take off with maximum horizontal speed and impact the maximum vertical velocity to the centre of gravity.

If these thoughts are compared with high jumpers who raise their centre of gravity over 1.30m in some cases, and sprinters who regularly run 11m per second speeds, we could have a very 'long' world record, metres beyond the present figure. As in most aspects of athletics, it is the words 'suitable personal compromises' which comes to the fore. The ability of an athlete to compromise in forward speed and vertical speed is the key area. Figures of two parts forward velocity to one vertical velocity have been mentioned but coaches need to be aware that it is a generalization. Individuals cope with the situation in varying ways. There is the essential need to maintain board contact time sufficiently to impart vertical lift to the body (centre of gravity).

One key area which can only assist the good vertical lift-off is the speed over the last 3-5 strides. This can be seen in the table of runway speeds compiled by Finnish scientists (Figure 3). There have been speeds in excess of 11mps achieved by men, and Heike Drechsler (Germany) has gone over 10mps.

If this were the only component of long jump, the majority of athletes would be in limbo. It is possible to train and coach athletes to achieve good final strides, even though they are not the best 100m runners in the world. To put the technical aspects in perspective it is necessary to break the jump into parts, as can be done for most events of a technical nature.

Running – Approach Run

Time spent on running techniques is never wasted on any event which has a high percentage of running in the whole. Too frequently athletes/coaches miss the basics of the event by wishing to move ahead too quickly. Taking the comparison of a 100m sprinter who can need up to 50m to achieve top velocity, most long jumpers require to reach a suitable optimum speed prior to this, with 'average run-ups' rarely exceeding 40 metres.

It must therefore become obvious that a suitable rhythm at optimum speed is an essential component of the approach run. It is neither essential, nor in most cases possible, for the athlete to attain maximum horizontal velocity for the whole run-up. It is therefore essential to develop a run-up speed curve to achieve the maximum controllable take-off velocity where the horizontal is converted to vertical. In some cases there is a very slight falling away of the maximum horizontal velocity as preparation for take-off occurs. The 'feeling' of the approach is essential. A mind/body rhythm is very important and not easy to achieve, as weather conditions can be

Figure 3

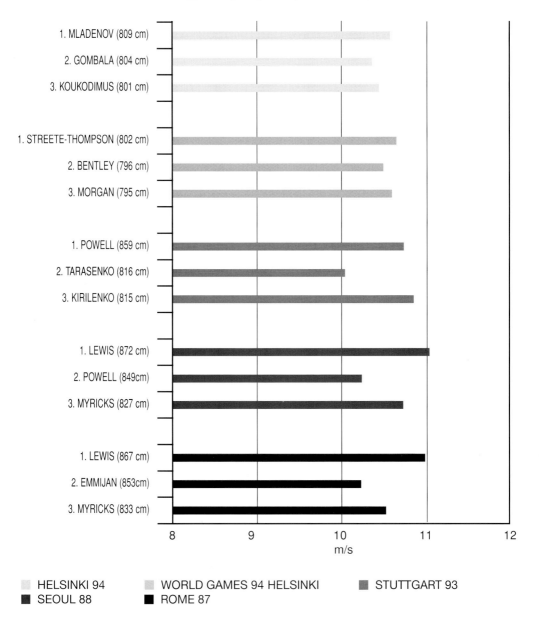

Long Jump: Speed (6m - > 1m)

Published by the Research Institute for Olympic Sports, Finland

a major factor both in preparation and in competition.

As can be seen in the table put together by scientists, the speed aspects of the approach require fast reaction, a high frequency of movements, and the ability to convert these aspects into special situations at take-off.

The visible overall expressions of speed, as is indicated on the tables, are all aspects of speed which are interconnected, but not directly interdependent. They all need to be developed, often in different ways. (Statistics indicate various parts of the run-up strides 11-6 etc.)

'Boardwork' - The Take Off

This next stage or component is very much inter-related with what has happened before, and there is far less time to do anything about mistakes. The preparation has been done in the final stages of the approach with the desired aim of maximising on explosive movement from the firm base of the board. The legs at this point are subjected to the

loading of the body as it prepares to run off an explosive leg position. If the leg is too straight the landing can be too much for most athletes. It is very much a compromise of the forward velocity with the ability to impart vertical velocity to the centre of gravity.

Here the conversion of a suitable running position (posture), the angle of take-off achieved, inter-related with the explosion of the leg muscles will determine the direction and distance of the jump. Other obvious components – free limbs the driving non take-off leg, the arms and the head position will all assist the take-off.

At the same time the hips have lowered slightly, and the legs have loaded (bent athletically, not straight or cocked) to create an explosive take-off (speed conversion). The initial slight sinking or lowering of the hips (pelvic area) is a difficult area to control, because there is of course the need to raise the region (centre of gravity) a stride later at the actual take-off. This can result in the next to last stride being slightly longer, but the last

Figure 4

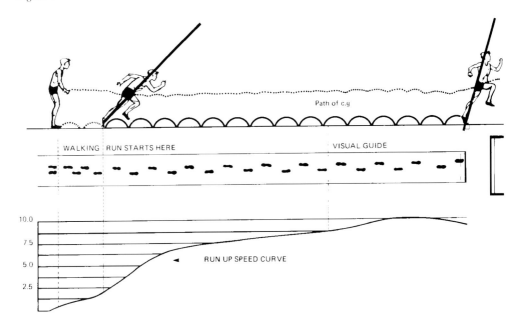

Figure 5
European Championships 1994 Helsinki
Long Jump – Men 10.08.94

No.	Name	1.	2.	3.	4.	5.	6.
837	Gombala Milan	10.25	10.12	9.98	10.18	10.08	10.04
	TCH	10.29	10.33	10.08	10.27	10.29	10.31
		785	804	783	779	602	783
		+1.1	+1.4	–0.5	–1.1	+0.5	–0.1
733	Bogryanov Dmitriy	10.33	10.08	10.27	10.04	10.22	10.16
	RUS	10.37	10.2	10.33	10.27	10.33	10.33
		788	0	785	0	0	796
		+1.0	–0.2	+0.1	–0.7	+1.5	–0.2
610	Campus Milko	10.16	10.22	10.18	—	—	—
	ITA	10.35	10.37	10.12	—	—	—
		776	0	0	—	—	—
		+1.0	+0.5	–0.2	—	—	—
824	Sunneborn Mattias	10.5	10.44	10.4	—	—	—
	SWE	10.68	10.64	10.53	—	—	—
		785	0	0	—	—	—
		+0.8	+0.4	+0.1	—	—	—
243	Mladenov Ivailo	10.4	10.68	10.33	10.33	10.59	10.46
	BUL	10.78	10.75	10.64	10.46	10.75	10.66
		802	0	778	788	794	809
		+1.4	+1.2	–0.6	–0.1	+1.1	–0.5
453	Ackermann Georg	10.53	10.71	10.29	—	—	—
	GER	10.48	10.62	10.55	—	—	—
		0	0	770	—	—	—
		-0.3	0.0	-0.8	—	—	—
218	Nijs Erik	10.33	10.53	10.27	10.25	10.2	10.14
	BEL	10.27	10.48	10.48	10.29	10.27	10.29
		783	0	789	771	770	772
		–0.2	+0.2	–1.2	–0.5	0.0	–0.5
526	Koukodimos Konstanti	10.33	10.35	10.18	10.31	9.88	10.31
	GRE	10.42	10.44	10.44	10.35	10.12	10.27
		0	0	801	0	0	0
		0.0	+1.4	+0.2	+0.4	–0.9	–0.4
730	Tudor Bogdan	10.35	10.29	10.2	10.14	—	10.18
	ROM	10.35	10.33	10.29	10.16	—	10.2
		799	797	776	752	0	768
		+1.7	+0.1	–1.1	0.0	—	0.8
227	Glavatskiy Aleksandr	10.1	10.16	10.06	—	—	—
	BLS	10.22	10.25	10.25	—	—	—
		782	0	0	—	—	—
		+0.8	+0.3	0.0	—	—	—
856	Kirilenko Vitaliy	10.35	9.86	9.88	10.25	9.96	10.42
	UKR	10.27	9.94	10	10.16	10.08	10.31
		755	788	0	792	0	0
		+0. 1	–0.2	–0.2	–0.6	+1.2	+0.3
771	Tarasenko Stanislav	10.22	10.29	9.92	9.9	10.18	10.42
	RUS	10.22	10.29	10.2	10.18	10	10.25
		780	793	0	0	787	0
		+0.4	–0. 1	+0.3	–0.4	–0.5	+0.3

Speed 1 : Between 11-6m   Speed 2 : Between 6-1m   Result   Wind Speed

Published by the Research Institute for Olympic Sports, Finland

stride on attacking distance shorter. To achieve the clawing onto the board, it can be up to 20cms shorter.

A reminder must be made that the hip sinking (pelvic adjustment) happens as part of the body awareness adjustment made in preparation for take-off. The building of confidence on the final strides must be done as part of the last 5 stride component, not in isolation. In many cases it happens as a natural response to take-off preparation, and athletes may be required to continue to run tall over the last strides to prevent too much sinking (they may need reminding often!). It is important to explain the increase of cadence and the running off and up from the board, rather than artificially teaching the sinking.

The actual leg/foot placements can best be seen in the photo sequences at the end of this book. It is equally visible in the sequences how the arms and driving leg help to continue that 'explosion' from the board. The free limbs also play a major part in balancing the tendency to over-rotate in a forward movement about the centre of gravity. If an athlete leans back at take-off much of the hard work and speed generated on the runway is lost, with a last stride which is too long. Vertical lift may increase, but with a reduced forward velocity distance is lost dramatically. As indicated by my colleagues in previous editions of this book, the use of a take-off ramp (raised take-off area) is very questionable for this aspect of training, though it may have value in giving 'airtime' for flight simulation. As in many areas of coaching it is important to realise what a particular activity is being used for

Airtime – Flight Patterns

A difficult area to give full credit to when there are many who still want to judge the long jump by how it looks. This is unfortunately an area where perhaps too much emphasis is placed on the aesthetics, rather than the facts – a poor technique done at speed and with lift will most likely still win over a pretty technique.

The key factor from the biomechanical point of view is that airtime movements can assist in correction of over-rotation – depending on the degree of the rotation – but these movements are not designed to affect the parabola of the centre of gravity which has been established at take-off. By using the legs it is possible to reduce the amount lost to forward rotation which will naturally bring the feet down early into the sand.

The rotation about the centre of gravity can be controlled and a type of backward displacement imposed on the body As can be seen in the photo sequences, the cyclic forward movement of legs and arms helps to absorb the forward rotation, and likewise helps to turn the trunk and hips backwards in the saggital plane.

It must be remembered at this point that certain techniques are not suitable for all long jumpers. If the athlete is achieving only 5m, the airtime is much reduced as compared with that available to an athlete with 8m potential. Here coaches need to fit the technique to the athlete, not the reverse. It is a very individual problem and frequently it is important to use the simplest technique. Progress to other techniques can occur as the young athlete generates more forward velocity, and is able to achieve a higher vertical component in the take-off.

It is women athletes who in recent years have given the best pointers to coaching the younger athletes, by achieving world record distances with 'stride' styles or modified sail techniques.

Touch Down – The Landing Phase

The athlete can make or break a jump by poor leg extension at landing. The feet then naturally drop under the body, and a standing position results. The technical aim of trying to get the heels as far ahead of the centre of gravity as possible does not always result in an extension of the distance of the final landing, because the athlete could well fall backwards. The high loss of forward speed at this stage of the jump has again to be optimised by the individual. If the athlete can arch the back as the heels touch and then collapse through the knees, there is a greater possibility of the main part of the body passing through the same hole made by the feet. Variations have developed with a skid through, but again much depends on the ability and agility of the athlete.

Whilst this chapter is only a brief look at the technical components of the jump, it could be useful to look at part of a table pulled together by scientists studying the components of long jump here in Great Britain. It summarises some of the ways that jumpers can achieve the basic aims of long jump – to jump a long way.

Figure 6

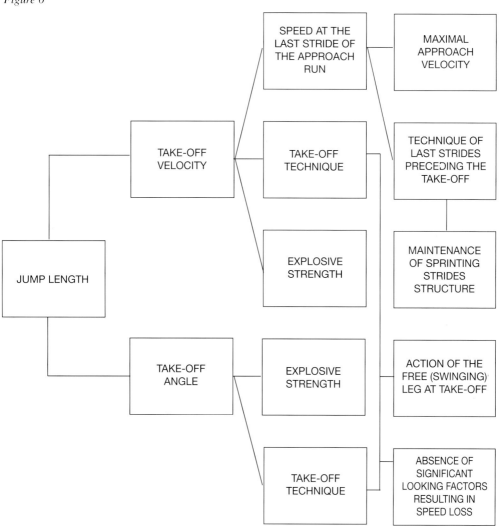

CHAPTER 4
The Technique of Long Jumping

As has been found in the previous chapters, the history of long jump has produced a number of variations in techniques used, from the early days of jumping with weights to taking off from ramps, and the last attempt to change the event by using a one-footed somersault. The latter was banned on the grounds of safety, but was perhaps the instigator of the greater use of biomechanical analysis: how we can ideally control the body and its parts (arms/legs/head) to take the best advantage.

Success in long jump is in fact determined by several important factors which appear in the lists for a number of events from hurdles to pole vault. The athlete needs to have:-

a. Speed – to produce a fast controlled approach
b. Strength – Power – which probably comes from the situation of strength divided by time
c. Agility – Co-ordination – the whole jump is one end product, but that is achieved by a co-ordinated series of activities
d. Strength – Durability – the take-off produces a short period of considerable stress.
e. Determination – as with most athletic events, the ideal result is not achieved overnight. Often years of practice, adjustment etc only scratch the surface of the athlete's ability.

The Approach

Athletes must strive to achieve a Maximum Controlled Velocity – Speed with control. If athletes can run faster as they approach the board, in theory they will jump further, though of course it is never quite as easy as that.

The major variations in an approach occur in most cases in the early stages – the acceleration phase. This means that there must be work done on the running technique of the athlete. Without doubt work devoted to sprinting and general running technique is time well spent for a long jumper. Arm action, knee pick-up, foot placement, head position – these are all areas where improvement will benefit the athlete, whether young or experienced.

Whilst being a good sprinter is without doubt beneficial, coaches must always remember the younger athletes may not have the strength in the early stages to handle all the factors required at one go.

Younger athletes can be judged for potential by a timed run over 20-25 metres which could be as far as they can handle full speed. Older athletes can be tested over 30-40 metres.

With these factors in mind how do you establish the approach? Whilst every athlete is an individual, there are a number of rule of thumb suggestions (age related)

Under 11	up to 11 strides
11 – 13	11 to 13 strides
13 – 15	13 to 15 strides
15 – 17	15 to 17 strides
Mature juniors & seniors	19 to 23 strides

The younger athletes would be wisest to use a standing start to provide at least one accurate mark between start and board. As an athlete becomes more advanced, there is a move toward a run on or walk on to the first check mark (CM). The use of odd number strides will allow the athlete to start with the take-off foot on the CM, a suitable routine for youngsters to develop. As with all aspects of technical events, the coach must be willing to adapt to what suits the athlete best.

As has been stated earlier, the length of the approach will be governed by the speed-strength ratio which will change as the athlete grows. On occasions it will reduce, especially if the athlete grows rapidly. Coaches need to monitor these changes, perhaps by a series of simple tests which can be incorporated into the training programme, often providing very interesting breaks in the routine of preparation.

Whatever approach an athlete and coach have decided is best, it must be accurately transferable from training environment to competition – either by a measuring tape, or by foot lengths (accurate heel to toe, same shoe as in training). Whenever changes are made to CMs, it must be remembered that markers are not allowed on the runway. They may be placed only alongside the runway and will often be official markers, not shoes. It is important for young athletes to compete in a known situation, rather than be upset at the start of a competition.

Approach Running

Having established that the ability to run well is important, what factors appear to stand out as important to the long jump approach? It must be repeated that these same factors are important in other events. This indicates the high inter-relationship of events, an important factor when considering the young athlete's development.

Running Technique – Posture

This will be dealt with in more detail in the chapter on teaching and coaching the long jump.

Speed

As indicated in earlier graphs, there are variations between the advanced athlete and the early learning athlete. The key is the application of speed at the vital correct time. Again this will vary according to the athlete's ability to handle the available speed.

After an early build-up of speed in the first 6 to 12 strides, according to the length of the run-up, there is an attempt to speed up the rate of striding over the last seven strides for seniors, perhaps five strides for novices.

During the last two strides the body has to adjust to create the platform from which to drive upwards and forwards. Whilst there may be a slight variation in speed, it is the aim to minimise this. The hips will start to sink naturally. This will happen and need not be emphasised when coaching. It explains why there is a slight speed loss. This is where the term maximum controlled velocity is a factor. The emphasis is on 'controlled', because the athlete is trying to achieve maximum suitable lift and keep control of speed.

Here the coaching point could be on attack and running through the take-off point into the flight phase. It is essential that the running technique is good; overstriding or backward lean will reduce the end result even before take-off. It is at this time that the athletes with the best technique gain the most, and often the point where the top sprinter-jumpers lose the most. The acquisition of speed and the control of that speed over the last strides is frequently demonstrated at major Games. Good jumping ability in most cases overcomes the flat out sprinter.

To achieve the ideal take-off position the athlete must 'feel' the approach. That feel is perhaps best described as rhythm, knowing naturally that the application point was correct. Here inexperience shows most with the young athlete who is slowing into the board. The practice and feel of an event is an obvious statement that is often overlooked in the rush to achieve a suitable end result; patience is a key to good coaching.

If an athlete can feel the run to be correct, then there becomes less and less necessity to have more than a starting CM and a cue mark for later in the approach.

Having established the factors which are involved in the Approach Run, what order you the coach put them in depends on the athlete. Perhaps the following might not suit a particular athlete: rhythm, running technique, speed, take-off, accuracy.

Whatever order is established in the coaching routine, it is essential that the athlete recognises these factors and the coach-athlete relationship is on the same wavelength.

How do we establish the Approach Accuracy?

1. It is essential to have a suitable practice run up before a competition.
2. It is essential that the established approach is suitable for the surface. Novice athletes can still learn their jumping on cinder runways at school. Today's synthetic surfaces allow much more accurate preparation
3. Start with take-off foot on the board. Run away from board for required number of strides. Place a CM.
4. Run the correct way down the runway to establish some basic accuracy. This will require two or more attempts to establish a suitable basic unit. The main feature at this stage is consistent running technique. Adjustments can be made easily in training (in competition there is often only time for two or three run-throughs for each athlete). A reminder about the running surface is important, as of course are weather conditions which will cause variations to occur: headwinds (slow down) – following winds (speed up).
5. Measure the approach (tape or foot lengths). Record the distance in the training diary, or even on the competition shoes, especially if you use the same shoes for training and competing.
6. The more experienced athletes may only have the one mark, but a 'cue mark' is allowed off the runway. Ensure that this is far enough away from take-off to allow concentration on the speed build-up.

Accuracy is achieved by training, application and more training!

The Long Jump

What do you do once the athlete has left the take-off board? This aspect in the past has had considerable time spent on it. Even today, there are some 'pretty jumpers' who look good, but do not go very far.

There is a basic equation on jumping long distance

SPEED (of approach) + Lift (at take-off)
+ Efficient landing = Distance

Good technique in the air will certainly affect one factor of the jump – the landing. What happens to the position of the body around the centre of gravity is important. Rotation will take place; how efficiently the athlete controls the forward rotation by use of arms, legs and head in flight is vital. However one important feature is that the novice athlete spends less time in the air than the expert. It is therefore important that a simple technique is adopted to suit the athlete. With speed advances, the athlete may wish to develop holding techniques to attempt the hold of the Centre of Gravity flight parabola for the optimum flight pattern.

For the novice the MISP method should be adopted: Make It Simple and Progressive.

Long Jump Flight Styles Examined

These techniques are not in any particular order, but without doubt the first three provide much more suitable starting points for the novice and developing athlete. It might be noted that the fifth technique is only used by the fastest sprinter/jumper athletes; why?– because it requires more 'air time'.

The Sail

This is the technique which the young athlete will almost certainly attempt without any real teaching or coaching. A good take-off position is achieved; then it is a case of tuck the knees up to the chest. The problem with this technique is that it creates rotation about the Centre of Gravity, and provides an almost impossible landing position. Not a technique to be encouraged beyond first attempts.

The Stride Jump

Over the last 15 years this technique has

Figure 7 – **The Stride Long Jump**

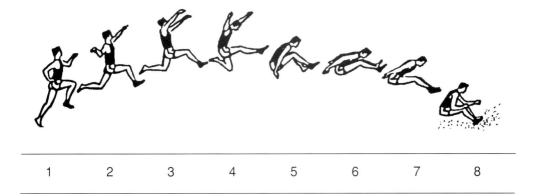

1	2	3	4	5	6	7	8

developed from an early introduction by former 'Eastern bloc' athletes, especially the female athletes. It is in fact a modification of the sail. However, instead of pulling the knees to the chest the athlete continues a good drive off the board. The free leg is driven into a position parallel with the ground with the foot held up, and thus a stride position is achieved. It is essential that the good upright body position is held for as long as possible. The arms are in a sprint type position at take-off. The arm which is back at drive off is brought through high to join the forward arm above head height. They then come down together close to the side of the body, while both legs are held out in front of the body for as long as possible. The arms come through at point of impact to encourage the Centre of Gravity to go forward and over the landing feet

The Hang
After a good take-off position has been achieved, the athlete drops the driving free leg to vertical where the take-off leg joins it in a long body position. The arms go high above the body to slow down the rotation about the Centre of Gravity. The long body (extension) increases the moment of inertia

about the transverse axis to create the slowing down of rotation. The landing requires a rapid jack-knife at the hips to create the angular velocity required to allow the legs to be lifted high. The arm action requires the arms to pass the Centre of Gravity to create hip thrust and leg shoot. See figure 8.

One of the problems of a hang technique is that athletes often fail to achieve a suitable take-off position and lose the hips before actually taking off. Some throw the head back, which of course only makes it more difficult to achieve the long high position required. An outstanding exponent of this technique in recent years has been the German long jumper Heike Drechsler.

The One Stride Hitchkick
A similar take-off position with the free thigh retaining the high position almost parallel with the ground. The leg is straightened and swung back and down as the take-off leg folds up beneath the hips and comes forward bent (see figure 9). The take-off leg continues its forward movement, straightening for landing and held as high as possible. The free leg completes its backward swing behind the hip (Centre of Gravity), then folds up and comes through bent to join the take-off leg for

Figure 8 – **The Hang**

| 1 | 2 | 3 | 4 | 5 | 6 | 7 | 8 | 9 |

landing. This technique is likely to prove an intermediate stage for top male jumpers capable of 8m plus as it is completed too soon. A long time is then spent holding the legs high to get the good leg shoot. There are two solutions to this 'problem': delay the action of the free leg thigh for longer (almost a stride jump position) before completing the leg action or learn a two stride hitchkick.

The Two Stride Hitchkick
A continuation of the 1 stride which attempts to delay forward rotation further. Having reached the high point in figure 9, the take-off leg – instead of waiting for the free leg to

come through – straightens and swings back. The free leg now comes through bent and straightens for landing. The stride is completed by the take-off leg coming through bent to join the free leg, thus continuing the running in the air.

It should be noted that in a hitchkick technique, forward leg movements are done flexed (bent) at the knee; the backwards movements are done with with straight positions – long legs. The arms move in sequence with the opposite leg and come together at landing. Wild use of the arms can cause considerable problems in flight creating a complete imbalance.

Figure 9 – **The One Stride Hitchkick**

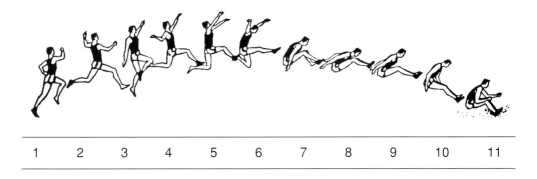

| 1 | 2 | 3 | 4 | 5 | 6 | 7 | 8 | 9 | 10 | 11 |

Teaching the Long Jump

The basics of the long jump are little more than a simple uncomplicated extension of good running. The problems can occur quickly due to complicating the procedure by introducing the advance model of board work too soon.

Begin by teaching the young athletes to run well with economy. Then allow them to think about speed and take-off as the climax to a good run.

The major 'problems' of basic long jumping is the fact that the young athlete very rarely has the necessary combination of speed, strength and co-ordination. Often only one of these factors is present in the early stages.

The early stages of long jump are normally introduced to groups of young athletes, so wherever possible this should be done with as many jumps as possible in a short time. Create the interest; nothing is worse than standing waiting for minutes for a run at the well dug sand.

The best planned sessions are those where the short approach is fixed by marker cones. It is important to have many jumps. A long approach only creates fatigue with the inexperienced unprepared young athlete. Seven strides are ample to produce a jump with whatever technique comes naturally. There are a number of basics (fundamentals) which can be introduced:
1. Run fast
2. Take-off: normal running position, head in line with spine. Therefore a flat back will occur.

Encourage a good driving knee position as in sprinting. If this is achieved a good extended take-off leg will occur.

If the young athlete can be encouraged to 'feel' the driving knee, then progress will occur.

Returning to the good running position will again encourage suitable use of the arms.

At this stage the actual take-off position relative to a board is not essential; the feeling is.

This particular phase of long jump is often

Figure 10

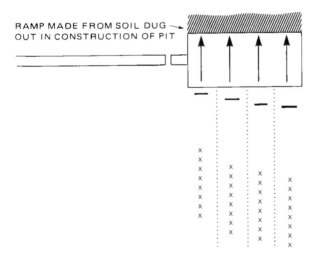

RAMP MADE FROM SOIL DUG OUT IN CONSTRUCTION OF PIT

rushed forward to get on to the real jumping; this frequently proves to be a trap once sprung never retracted.

There are natural techniques in running which are essential; there is no way back for many young athletes who try to stub their foot into the board when the natural progression is fast footed pawing or clawing of the take-off foot. It *must* be natural for the young athlete to run over the board with an active foot, not one which stubs the board in an almost stopping action.

1. Normal head position looking ahead, perhaps at a predetermined sighting – not upwards.
2. Flat back
3. Good extending take-off leg
4. Driving free leg
5. Good sprint arm action
6. Extending active foot

When the board is introduced to the young athlete there will be many who plant the foot incorrectly by aiming to have a flat foot. Figure 11 indicates how it should be a rolling action where the heel of the foot lands slightly first and there is an active rolling action through to a good extension.

At this early stage it is possible to 'spot' the basic problem of stepping away from the central position, see figure 12.

At these early stages of learning the correct take-off position there should be no pressure on what the athlete does immediately after

take-off. Let it develop naturally, one stage at a time.

Good running (speedy) into good take-off (active).

If a good take-off position is achieved, then the young athletes will jump a relatively long way. To allow a breathing space for them to think, the next thing they can probably be aware of is a suitable landing with legs out in front. How they get them there at this stage is interesting to the coach/teacher, but perhaps best noted and not commented on.

It can be pointed out to the young athletes at this stage that the active driving take-off foot position is also important to their hurdles and sprinting, a multi-event approach which could well benefit their athletic-long jump progress in the future.

When Do You Teach The Air Techniques? Where? How?

A question frequently asked by thoughtful coaches/teachers.

These techniques can be taught in a gymnasium using soft mats which do not move on landing! - or of course into a normal long jump pit outdoors. Whilst a ramp/beat board may be used to give more air time, there can be negative aspects where incorrect foot placements will create artificial and incorrect habits at take-off. One solution used has been a flat raised ramp up to 10cm high; on this the clawing action is encouraged in

Figure 11

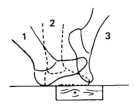

Figure 12

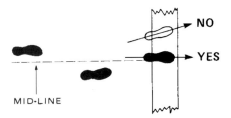

correct position, though of course earlier than normal.

Whatever artificial methods are used the coach/teacher should return to normality as soon as possible to prevent poor habits forming. The alternative could be that athletes jump from normal take-off into lower sand, thus giving more time for the air activity.

As indicated, there are many young athletes who will not progress much beyond the basic active take-off. For those who wish to progress and use the basic points to an advantage perhaps the stride jump is the best first stage technique to progress to. It has been used very successfully by many female athletes over the last ten years, including various World Record holders.

The Stride Jump *(See Figure 7)*
In a class situation the activities can be as follows:
1.	Good take-off position. Hold free thigh in high position; land in a split position.
2.	Carry out point 1, then bring take-off leg through to join free leg at landing.
3.	Progress to holding both legs as high as possible for as long as possible, therefore reaching with the feet ahead of the body.
4.	Repeat point 3 and ensure the arms are now being brought into the action correctly. Remembers one point at a time; legs, then arms. Some things happen naturally; allow them to do so.

The Hang *(See Figure 8)*
1.	Progress as from stride jump approach. Ensure the athletes take off actively and do not lose their hips at take-off.
2.	Learning to drop the free leg to join the take-off leg and create the long position.
3.	When long position is achieved, fold both legs underneath the body.
4.	Finally, aim to bring the legs through held as high as possible ready for contact with the sand.
5.	The arms after take-off will have been held high and back, ready to sweep through from behind the hips, which should assist the Centre of Gravity (body mass) to move forwards over the feet during landing.

Whilst there may be opportunities for teaching the Hitchkick style, in most cases this will be done with the more advanced athlete – very rarely, if ever, with a young athlete.

It will be a case of where does teaching stop and advanced coaching start. Perhaps here it would be best to say that the learning of this style of jumping requires much more air time and technical time on an individual basis. Probably a gymnasium with ramps or high bar or even a foam pit are the more suitable learning centres.

The major factor to learn is the bent knee drive forward and up, followed by straighter leg sweeps backwards with the rear leg.

Figure 9 gives the action required.

CHAPTER SIX
Training for Long Jump

This particular chapter has the aim of providing ideas and starting points for coaches and athletes. It is by no means an exhaustive list of everything which can be done to get athletes fit to produce their best at any particular competition.

The very nature of our sport means that we can only generalise our ideas. How these ideas are interpreted is very individual, as no two athletes are exactly the same in their ability, what they would like to achieve, and what they can achieve. The aim of an individual's training must be to get fit. How these ideas, training guidelines and support activities are used is coaching, and the skill of the coach will show through.

Training Sessions

There must be a simple, logical pattern which can be easily followed by the novice or advanced jumper. It should suit the facilities available and the time the athlete has available. If the athlete is interested and keen to learn, and in the case of the older athlete motivated to go on progressing, then they will arrive on time and ready to go whenever possible.

A basic session could follow the routine:
1. Warm Up – Jog for 4-8 minutes. It is not necessary to go round and round a track. In fact this is probably better done away from the track by young athletes.
2 General mobility exercises which are not long jump specific, but start at the neck, then shoulders, trunk, then legs/ankles.
3. Specific mobility exercises as shown later in this chapter (figures 26-32) are just a selection of those which can be used for long jumping.
4. Strides and running technique, followed by long jump technique.
5. Fitness work. For young athletes this can be group relay activities. Fun work can be hard work.

6. Warm down – easy jog.

This can, and should, frequently be followed by a simple evaluation of the work done by advanced athletes, and a brief reminder of points covered by the younger athlete to provide aims for next time.

Planning the Training of a Committed Athlete

This type of planning is not possible with younger athletes; they may be long jumping as part of an overall athletic programme. However it is hoped that as athletes become committed to their event, they will eventually feel it is essential to have a structured training programme which is planned a year ahead.

We must always remember that athletics is an all-year activity, and committed athletes will always want to know the pattern of their preparation and where it is going. There will again be many ways forward depending on the stage the athlete has reached at the end of the previous season. This will mean varying skill levels have to be fitted in and seasonal aims (peaks) for the next year decided, all of which fits into a general pattern of planning of:

Preparation, 1 & 2, Pre-Competition, 2/3, and Competition – and then, of course, regeneration before the next winter training.

A general term used has been Periodisation of the year – either a simple one where summer is the aim, or double where the athlete wishes to compete indoors in the February/March period, then return to further preparation for the summer.

The theory of periodisation – the division of specific training periods – is to be found in the BAF book on Training Theory. It will be seen from the explanation there that it is aimed at a systematic, well organised preparation of the athlete's training, which cannot be anything but good for the athlete and coach to follow. However it must always be remembered that all the best laid plans can go wrong. The coach and athlete always need to be realistic in their applications of what they have established at the beginning of the winter.

In general terms, the periodising of an

Figure 13

Single Periodised Year:

Months	Nov	Dec	Jan	Feb	Mar	Apr	May	Jun	Jul	Aug	Sep	Oct
Phases	1				2			3		4	5	6
Periods	preparation						competition					regener-ation

Figure 14

Double Periodised Year:

Months	Nov	Dec	Jan	Feb	Mar	Apr	May	Jun	Jul	Aug	Sep	Oct
Phases	1_1		2_1	3_1	1_2	2_2	3_2	4			5	6
Periods	preparation			comp.	preparation		competition					regener-ation

athlete's training year is rather like building a pyramid. It is essential to have a good firm broad base of training onto which can be built many variations. The first part of winter training needs to have the real slog work of the programme, whilst still providing interest and incentives. Here the athlete will gradually build up the volume of work, though the intensity of any quality needs to be well controlled.

Quite obviously, as winter progresses the quality and speed of work will improve. It is during this phase of training that the coach and athlete need to know the level they have reached and be constantly aware of the improvement levels.

The Young Athlete

When looking at workloads it is essential that the coach and athlete are fully aware that with younger athletes it is not just a matter of

scaling down the training programme carried out by a senior athlete. It is vital that all aspects of a child's development are considered. Growth patterns involving height and weight are very important guides to the actual workload undertaken. Equally so are the types of training, especially those involving the exposure of young athletes to anaerobic activities. These should be left out altogether in the early years. When introduced later a very close watch on progress/improvement needs to be maintained.

It cannot be stated strongly enough that the introduction of strength training is another area which needs to be very closely monitored. A young athlete who is growing rapidly has a number of very vulnerable areas, in particular the growing ends of the bones and the spine. These are the areas which would take the strain if overloaded with heavy weight training bars. It is possible to work the immature body well by using light sessions of hopping and bounding, circuits, medicine ball work and body-weight activities, all of which will build the specific jumping strength required, whilst the circuit will develop the strength endurance relevant to the particular level of the young athlete.

Whatever the level of the athlete, it must be recognised that training schedules should be designed so that they move from general work to specifics – from preparation to competition phases. The whole process need not be complicated. The main feature should always be that each athlete is an individual. Everyone has strengths and weaknesses; the skill of coaching is how these are balanced out over the programme. It is essential that the progressions are notable, and for all athletes it should be challenging and enjoyable.

To actually establish the criteria, coaches could think along the following lines:
1. Identify the next season's aims.
2. Qualify when the most important periods are.
3. Establish the various units:
   a. Early Winter Preparation
   b. Second Phase of Winter
   c. Pre-Competition
   d. Peak Periods
   f. Possible easier periods during the competition phase.
   g. Recovery – Regeneration
4. Identify the types of fitness required in particular periods.
5. How it is possible to achieve that fitness.
6. Look at the time available to the athlete at various stages of the year – exams etc.
7. Put all the ideas together and, where appropriate, discuss with the athlete; or, with younger athletes, explain what you are trying to do – SIMPLY.

The following principles are aspects which are recommended as part of all training programmes:

1. Running Endurance

These activities are aimed at becoming cardio-vascular efficient. It most certainly helps the legs to get basic conditioning.
(a) Steady rate running (approximately 150 heart beats per min). The methods to achieve this aspect vary from coach to coach.

Obviously what is a long way for some athletes is no problem to others. The use of good grass surfaces for these workloads should be a priority to prevent early soreness and injuries. Anything from 5-8 minutes for a young athlete to 30 minutes for a mature athlete are the foundations of this type of work.
(b) Interval running (as indicated in the Middle Distance books) will indicate 10 x 'x' with 'y' seconds recovery which can be gradually developed through the preparation period by (i) reducing the recovery, (ii) increasing the speed, (iii) increasing the reps.

The problem which appears to occur with technical event athletes is that this can be boring. Try varying the lengths of the runs in sessions 200-180-160 x 2 etc. This can help, as can varied environments. Relays: continuous in 3, 5, 7s etc makes it more fun. Monotony kills the enthusiasm very quickly.
(c) The use of Fartlek Training, if done correctly, can be equally challenging to the jumpers. Varying the distances of faster efforts will increase the intensity of training, yet still provide interest. Changing the venues for such training can again provide the stimulating effect required by athletes.

2. Strength Endurance

This is for the more mature athlete. It has been defined as "the capacity to maintain the quality of the muscle's contractile force, in the climate of endurance." There are many ways to produce this aspect of training. The variation will depend on the area in which the athlete resides, and equally on the imagination of the coach to motivate the athlete to try:
(a) Sand hill running – varying courses.
(b) Hill runs – 70-90m x 4 through to 150m x 4 x 2 etc are all possible. Jog backs can be introduced after the athlete has achieved a certain level on walk back etc.
(c) Back to Backs – higher quality running over shorter distances with shorter recoveries all provide variety.

(d) Harness running – a useful variation, but it must be remembered that the person providing the resistance needs to be sensible. This activity may not be the most suitable for young athletes who are not aware of their own strengths.

(e) Tyre pulling – weighting the tyre according to ability makes this a more controllable method of resistance.

There are many other ways of providing strength endurance activities for the younger athletes by using their own body weight or that of partners. It can be hard but fun.

3. Speed Endurance

This is defined as "the capacity for co-ordinating the speed of contraction of the muscles in a climate of endurance."

Whilst a jumper may not require too much of this in a competition, where the approach is only 20-40m, it is an important part of the ability to run well with suitable rhythm.

(a) Runs of quality, 60-120m with full recovery, provide suitable work.

(b) Acceleration runs with a 'speed play' element – the ability to accelerate-decelerate-accelerate. 2 sets of 4-8 runs will provide suitable work.

This type of work needs to be done on good surfaces – track or good grass.

4. Pure Speed

As has been indicated earlier, the need for basic speed and runway specific speed has been mentioned frequently. If the male athlete does not have a 10.50 for 100m or 6.75/80 for 60m indoors, or the female athlete is slower than 11.50 and 7.35, there is no reason to despair, mainly because there are many activities which can develop speed:

(a) Runway sprinting

(b) Acceleration runs done over 50-80m using the rhythm of accelerate, sprint fast, decelerate. The 50m is closely related to the actual runway work, and can be adapted as part of mind games preparation (competition preparation).

(c) Accuracy runs. These must always have a take-off at the end, otherwise they are irrelevant. The rhythm required is essentially different if a take-off has to be executed at the end of the run.

All this work is quality and not quantity; therefore full recovery is required, and the number of reps must be controlled to achieve the quality.

5. Strength

This is normally defined as 'the ability to exert force against resistance." Quite obviously, the type of force and the type of resistance will vary from event to event.

The judgement required to decide the training role of specificity will decide what the coach is looking for in each individual's development. The broad divisions of types of strength are covered mainly by maximum, endurance strength and elastic. The latter is obviously very high on the list of priorities for long jumping. As was indicated in the technical aspects of long jump, if there is a high level of elastic strength there should be a fair ability to impart a high vertical velocity to the centre of gravity at take-off.

As previously indicated, strength endurance is high on the list of preparation work, establishing the foundation on which to build the complete jump.

Maximum Strength

This is required by long jumpers, obviously not in such amounts as required by the throwers, but certainly much more than by the endurance runner. This area figures much higher in the list of priorities for an experienced mature jumper than it does for a novice.

Endurance Strength

The 'capacity to withstand fatigue' is an important feature in the preparation period and needs to be maintained during the competition period. Circuit training and its many variations are most useful. It is possible

Fitness programmes today can be simple or sophisticated, as is shown by the following exercises – all of which are but a selection of those available to the coach.

Figure 15 – 'V' sit

Figure 18 – Back extension

Figure 16 – Star jumps

Figure 19 – Leg change

Figure 17 – Push-ups

Figure 20 – Sit-ups

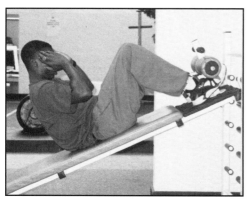

Figure 21 – Inclined sit-up

Figure 24 – Quadricep curl

Figure 22 – Leg Press machine

Figure 25 – Back raise

Figure 23 – Hamstring curl

to put greater emphasis on the legs where required in such workouts.

Whilst the main aim of a 'circuit' is to cover all muscle groups, there are specific circuits which can increase the overload as and when required. Variations can be brought about by:

increasing the number of reps
decreasing the intervals of rest
increasing the number of circuits
    undertaken.

One variation of a jumper's circuit is included in the Appendix at the end of this book.

Elastic Strength

Here the aim is to improve the elastic and contractile components of the muscle. These components are developed by reflex contractions in the expression of strength at speed. The best known and most widely used methods to develop this type of strength are:

(a)   Hopping, bounding and other multiple jumping activities (plyometric work)
(b)   Weight training with free weights
(c)   Combinations of the above, according to the individual's needs.

Hopping, Bounding and Multiple Jumping – Plyometric Work

Whilst this is a well known method of preparation, it is often a much abused method. Teaching of the required technique is an essential. It is also very important for the coach to observe the sessions, especially with young athletes. As athletes mature it becomes of less importance, but it is still useful to observe. Another important feature is the surface on which this work is carried out. It is best done away from the synthetic track; good grass surfaces are perhaps the best, or protected floors (thin rubber cover, not deep mats).

Early stages need to emphasise:

(a)   Foot contact – reaching and pawing action of a flat foot (not heavy heel contacts)
(b)   Upright body – trunk and head

(c)   Hips in line – no bottoms stuck out!
(d)   Good arm action – alternate arms.

The development of the programme can hinge on various permutations of hops, steps and jumps. The learning process provides a fun element for the younger athlete. The more experienced athlete often becomes competitive, especially when training in groups. Whilst this has a place on occasions, it does often become a case of technique being forgotten, and injury invited in!

With young athletes, it is recommended that the early activities are two footed jumps until the body can handle the pressure of repeated single leg activities.

It must also be remembered that these activities are quite hard for the younger athletes, and are well avoided in the early stages of the preparation period. There is a need to have a level of fitness before introducing this work; therefore it is not recommended as a method to get fit initially.

A useful method of controlling the training is being aware of how many contacts an athlete does in a session. Likewise, how many contacts the athlete can handle in each effort before the technique starts to break down.

Where these activities are used as a means to maintain fitness during the competition period, it is recommended that the number of contacts is reduced and the emphasis is on speed and quick reactions.

Developments in the plyometric field (depth jumping using body weight, using weighted jackets etc) are very much the area of the experienced athlete and have no place in a novice's programme. Even where used with advanced athletes, care must be taken with the increases in body weight (jackets). 5% over natural body weight can be used as a rule of thumb. Variations using box tops, hurdles or stadium steps are all local activities the coach can develop, as are specific bounding box sets using boxes of varying heights over a set distance etc.

The young athlete needs protection from

over exposure to the more advanced exercises. Progress very gradually towards the inclusion of 'harder' variations from winter to winter rather than week to week. A very broad sensible base is required by the young athlete; it can take years – be patient! Fun circuits and drills are important to the youngster, not complete fatigue.

A series of drills and practices for ADVANCED ATHLETES is included in the Appendix section at the end of this book.

Weight Training (free bars and discs)

This is a very specialist area which is covered in a separate BAF book. It is an activity which needs to be done properly and safely, requiring qualified expert instruction with continued evaluation. Major damage can be done by too early an introduction to heavy levels of loading. Instruction on the correct methods of lifting can be given by using just a bar and wooden discs. In the earlier years the feature can be endurance based rather than high quantity.

6. Mobility

A supple athlete is one who has some protection from injury. General activities can be included in every training session prior to specialist long jump exercises. Some of these are shown in the next few pages. They are not an exhaustive list, just a selection. There are many variations and additions shown in the BAF book "Mobility Training" and a number of other specialist books available.

It must be remembered that for beginners and for most athletes the stretching should be of the slow stretch nature, not the ballistic (bounce) type. Suggestions vary according to experts and changing opinions. However the most common regime does agree on a slow stretch for 10-15 seconds, hold, press again, hold and relax, with the number of reps varying according to age and ability.

Figure 26 – Touching the toes

Figure 27 – Hamstring stretch

Figure 28 – Hurdler's stretch

Figure 29 – Shin/Quad stretch

Figure 30 – Ballistic bar stretch

Figure 31 – The Plough

Figure 32 – **Long Jump Sample Mobility Session**

TABLE A: JUMPS DECATHLON SCORING TABLES

The tables were compiled graphically and extended to cover the lower ability ranges. Approximations were made in some cases to prevent fractions of a cm. from coming in to the scale. In all events except the five stride long jump the mean was taken from test results obtained from non-specialist groups at Young Athletes Courses. In most the top mark is that of the approximate world record for the event, mainly set by professional jumpers of the late eighteen hundreds. The mean for the five stride long jump is taken from tests given to specialist jumpers. Hence the tables cannot be used to compare one leaping event with another. Their main aim is to encourage leaping and bounding as an enjoyable means of training for other events with a little direct and indirect competition as an added incentive. The events are not necessarily listed in the best order.

Standing Broad Jump; Both feet together; arms can be used to aid lift. Measurement to nearest point of contact.

Points	1 Stand Long Jump	2 Stand Triple Jump	3 2 Hops Step & Jump	4 2 Hops 2 Steps & Jump	5 2 Hops 2 Steps 2 Jumps	6 5 Spring Jumps	7 Stand 4 Hops & Jump	8 Run 4 Hops & Jump	9 25 Metre Hop in secs	10 5 Stride Long Jump
100	3.73m	10.51m	13.00m	15.54m	19.15m	17.06m	17.67m	23.77m	2.7	7.28m
99	–	10.43m	12.90m	15.46m	18.99m	16.91m	17.52m	23.62m	–	–
98	3.65m	10.36m	12.80m	15.39m	18.84m	16.76m	17.37m	23.46m	2.8	–
97	–	10.28m	12.69m	15.31m	18.69m	16.61m	17.22m	23.31m	–	7.26m
96	3.58m	10.21m	12.59m	15.08m	18.54m	16.45m	17.06m	23.16m	3.0	–
95	–	10.13m	12.49m	15.01m	18.38m	16.40m	16.96m	23.01m	–	–
94	3.50m	10.05m	12.39m	14.88m	18.23m	16.25m	16.86m	22.85m	3.1	7.23m
93	–	9.98m	12.29m	14.78m	18.08m	16.15m	16.76m	22.70m	–	–
92	3.42m	9.90m	12.19m	14.68m	17.93m	16.00m	16.61m	22.55m	3.2	–
91	–	9.82m	12.09m	14.57m	17.77m	15.84m	16.45m	22.35m	–	7.21m
90	3.35m	9.75m	11.98m	14.47m	17.62m	15.79m	16.35m	21.99m	3.3	–
89	–	9.68m	11.88m	14.37m	17.47m	15.64m	16.25m	21.79m	–	–
88	3.27m	9.60m	11.78m	14.27m	17.32m	15.54m	16.15m	21.64m	3.4	7.18m
87	–	9.52m	11.68m	14.17m	17.17m	15.39m	16.00m	21.48m	–	–
86	3.20m	9.44m	11.58m	14.07m	17.01m	15.23m	15.84m	21.33m	3.5	–
85	–	9.37m	11.48m	13.96m	16.91m	15.18m	15.74m	21.18m	–	7.16m
84	3.12m	9.29m	11.37m	13.86m	16.76m	15.03m	15.64m	21.03m	3.6	–
83	–	9.22m	11.27m	13.76m	16.66m	14.93m	15.54m	20.80m	3.7	7.13m
82	3.04m	9.14m	11.17m	13.66m	16.50m	14.83m	15.44m	20.65m	3.8	–
81	–	9.06m	11.07m	13.56m	16.35m	14.68m	15.34m	20.42m	3.9	7.11m
80	2.97m	8.99m	10.97m	13.46m	16.20m	14.57m	15.23m	20.26m	4.0	–
79	–	8.91m	10.87m	13.36m	16.10m	14.42m	15.08m	20.11m	4.2	7.08m
78	2.89m	8.83m	10.76m	13.25m	16.00m	14.32m	14.93m	19.96m	4.3	–
77	–	8.76m	10.66m	13.15m	15.84m	14.22m	14.83m	19.81m	4.4	7.06m
76	2.81m	8.68m	10.56m	13.05m	15.69m	14.07m	14.73m	19.58m	4.5	7.03m
75	–	8.61m	10.46m	12.95m	15.54m	13.96m	14.63m	19.43m	4.6	7.01m
74	2.74m	8.53m	10.36m	12.85m	15.39m	13.86m	14.47m	19.20m	4.7	6.95m
73	2.69m	8.45m	10.26m	12.75m	15.23m	13.71m	14.32m	19.04m	4.8	6.90m
72	2.66m	8.38m	10.15m	12.64m	15.13m	13.61m	14.22m	18.89m	4.9	6.85m
71	2.64m	8.30m	10.05m	12.49m	15.03m	13.51m	14.12m	18.74m	5.0	6.80m
70	2.61m	8.22m	9.95m	12.42m	14.88m	13.41m	14.02m	18.59m	5.1	6.75m
69	2.59m	8.15m	9.85m	12.34m	14.73m	13.25m	13.86m	18.44m	5.2	6.70m
68	2.56m	8.07m	9.75m	12.19m	14.63m	13.10m	13.71m	18.28m	5.4	6.62m
67	2.53m	8.00m	9.65m	12.09m	14.47m	13.00m	13.61m	18.13m	5.5	6.55m
66	2.51m	7.92m	9.55m	11.98m	14.32m	12.90m	13.51m	17.98m	5.6	6.47m
65	2.48m	7.84m	9.44m	11.88m	14.22m	12.80m	13.41m	17.75m	5.7	6.40m
64	2.46m	7.77m	9.34m	11.78m	14.07m	12.69m	13.30m	17.60m	5.8	6.32m
63	2.43m	7.69m	9.24m	11.68m	13.96m	12.59m	13.20m	17.37m	5.9	6.24m
62	2.41m	7.61m	9.14m	11.58m	13.81m	12.49m	13.10m	17.22m	6.0	6.17m
61	2.38m	7.54m	9.04m	11.48m	13.71m	12.34m	12.95m	17.06m	6.1	6.09m
60	2.36m	7.46m	8.94m	11.37m	13.56m	12.19m	12.80m	16.91m	6.2	6.01m
59	2.33m	7.39m	8.83m	11.27m	13.41m	12.03m	12.64m	16.76m	6.3	5.94m
58	2.31m	7.31m	8.73m	11.17m	13.25m	11.88m	12.49m	16.53m	6.5	5.86m
57	2.28m	7.23m	8.63m	11.07m	13.10m	11.78m	12.39m	16.38m	6.6	5.79m
56	2.26m	7.16m	8.53m	10.97m	12.95m	11.68m	12.29m	16.15m	6.7	5.71m
55	2.23m	7.08m	8.45m	10.87m	12.80m	11.58m	12.19m	16.00m	6.8	5.63m
54	2.20m	7.01m	8.38m	10.76m	12.64m	11.48m	12.09m	15.84m	6.9	5.56m
53	2.18m	6.93m	8.30m	10.66m	12.49m	11.37m	11.98m	15.69m	7.0	5.48m
52	2.15m	6.85m	8.22m	10.56m	12.34m	11.27m	11.58m	15.54m	7.1	5.41m
51	2.13m	6.78m	8.15m	10.46m	12.19m	11.17m	11.42m	15.39m	7.2	5.33m
50	2.10m	6.70m	8.07m	10.36m	12.03m	11.07m	11.27m	15.23m	7.3	5.25m

Standing Triple: Take-off foot to remain in flat contact with the ground, although free swinging on non-contact leg can be used. The same rule applies to the other three three hop, step and jump combinations.

Two hops, two steps, two jumps: The second of the two jumps is made from a two foot take-off.

Five Spring Jumps: Five successive two foot bounds. The feet must be kept together and the movement must be continuous.

Standing Four Hops and a Jump: Start as for standing triple. Tables compiled for dominant leg.

Running Four Hops and a Jump. Length of run unlimited.

25m Hop: From standing position. Tables compiled for dominant leg, although the mean of the left and right should be the recorded performance.

Five Stride Long Jump: Normal jumping rules, except that the run is limited to five strides.

Most of the events are educable and improve with training. All ten events, allowing two or three successful attempts at each, is a good single training session for any power-thirsty athlete.

Points	1 Stand Long Jump	2 Stand Triple Jump	3 2 Hops Step & Jump	4 2 Hops 2 Steps & Jump	5 2 Hops 2 Steps 2 Jumps	6 5 Spring Jumps	7 Stand 4 Hops & Jump	8 Run 4 Hops & Jump	9 25 Metre Hop in secs	10 5 Stride Long Jump
49	2.08m	6.62m	8.00m	10.26m	11.88m	10.97m	11.17m	15.08m	7.4	5.18m
48	2.05m	6.55m	7.92m	10.15m	11.73m	10.87m	11.07m	14.93m	–	5.13m
47	2.03m	6.47m	7.84m	10.05m	11.58m	10.76m	10.97m	14.78m	7.5	5.07m
46	2.00m	6.40m	7.77m	9.95m	11.42m	10.66m	10.82m	14.63m	–	5.02m
45	1.98m	6.32m	7.69m	9.85m	11.27m	10.56m	10.66m	14.47m	7.7	4.97m
44	1.95m	6.24m	7.61m	9.75m	11.17m	10.46m	10.51m	14.32m	–	4.92m
43	1.93m	6.17m	7.54m	9.65m	11.07m	10.36m	10.36m	14.17m	7.8	4.87m
42	1.90m	6.09m	7.46m	9.55m	10.97m	10.26m	10.21m	14.02m	–	4.82m
41	1.87m	6.01m	7.39m	9.44m	10.87m	10.15m	10.05m	13.86m	7.9	4.77m
40	1.85m	5.94m	7.31m	9.34m	10.76m	10.05m	9.90m	13.71m	–	4.72m
39	1.82m	5.86m	7.23m	9.24m	10.66m	9.95m	9.75m	13.56m	8.0	4.67m
38	1.80m	5.79m	7.16m	9.14m	10.56m	9.85m	9.60m	13.41m	–	4.62m
37	1.77m	5.71m	7.08m	9.04m	10.46m	9.75m	9.44m	13.25m	8.1	4.57m
36	1.75m	5.63m	7.01m	8.94m	10.36m	9.65m	9.34m	13.10m	–	4.52m
35	1.72m	5.56m	6.93m	8.83m	10.26m	9.55m	9.24m	12.95m	8.2	4.47m
34	1.70m	5.48m	6.85m	8.73m	10.15m	9.44m	9.14m	12.80m	–	4.41m
33	1.67m	5.41m	6.78m	8.63m	10.05m	9.34m	9.04m	12.64m	8.3	4.36m
32	1.65m	5.33m	6.70m	8.53m	9.95m	9.24m	8.94m	12.49m	–	4.31m
31	1.62m	5.25m	6.62m	8.43m	9.85m	9.14m	8.83m	12.34m	8.4	4.26m
30	1.60m	5.18m	6.55m	8.33m	9.75m	9.04m	8.73m	12.19m	–	4.21m
29	1.57m	5.10m	6.47m	8.22m	9.65m	8.94m	8.63m	12.03m	8.5	4.16m
28	1.54m	5.02m	6.40m	8.12m	9.55m	8.83m	8.53m	11.88m	–	4.11m
27	1.52m	4.95m	6.32m	8.02m	9.44m	8.73m	8.43m	11.73m	8.6	4.06m
26	1.49m	4.87m	6.24m	7.92m	9.34m	8.63m	8.33m	11.58m	–	4.01m
25	1.47m	4.80m	6.17m	7.82m	9.24m	8.53m	8.22m	11.42m	8.7	3.96m
24	1.44m	4.72m	6.09m	7.72m	9.14m	8.43m	8.12m	11.27m	–	3.91m
23	1.42m	4.64m	5.99m	7.61m	9.04m	8.33m	8.02m	11.12m	–	3.86m
22	1.39m	4.57m	5.89m	7.51m	8.94m	8.22m	7.92m	10.97m	8.9	3.80m
21	1.37m	4.49m	5.79m	7.41m	8.83m	8.12m	7.82m	10.82m	–	3.75m
20	1.34m	4.41m	5.68m	7.31m	8.73m	8.02m	7.72m	10.66m	–	3.70m
19	1.29m	4.26m	5.58m	7.21m	8.63m	7.92m	7.61m	10.51m	9.0	3.65m
18	1.26m	4.19m	5.48m	7.11m	8.53m	7.82m	7.51m	10.36m	–	3.60m
17	1.24m	4.11m	5.38m	7.01m	8.43m	7.72m	7.41m	10.21m	–	3.55m
16	1.21m	4.03m	5.28m	6.90m	8.33m	7.61m	7.31m	10.05m	9.1	3.50m
15	1.19m	3.96m	5.18m	6.80m	8.22m	7.51m	7.21m	9.90m	–	3.45m
14	1.16m	3.88m	5.07m	6.70m	8.12m	7.41m	7.11m	9.75m	·	3.40m
13	1.14m	3.80m	4.97m	6.60m	8.02m	7.31m	7.01m	9.60m	9.2	3.35m
12	1.11m	3.73m	4.87m	6.50m	7.92m	7.21m	6.90m	9.44m	·	3.25m
11	1.09m	3.65m	4.77m	6.40m	7.82m	7.11m	6.80m	9.29m	–	3.14m
10	1.06m	3.58m	4.67m	6.29m	7.72m	7.01m	6.70m	9.14m	9.3	3.04m
9	1.04m	3.50m	4.57m	6.19m	7.61m	6.90m	6.60m	8.99m	·	2.94m
8	1.01m	3.42m	4.47m	6.09m	7.51m	6.80m	6.50m	8.83m	–	2.84m
7	0.99m	3.35m	4.36m	5.99m	7.41m	6.70m	6.40m	8.68m	9.4	2.74m
6	0.96m	3.27m	4.26m	5.89m	7.31m	6.60m	6.29m	8.53m	–	2.64m
5	0.93m	3.20m	4.16m	5.79m	7.21m	6.50m	6.19m	8.38m	–	2.53m
4	0.91m	3.12m	4.06m	5.68m	7.11m	6.40m	6.09m	8.22m	9.5	2.43m
3	0.88m	3.04m	3.96m	5.58m	7.01m	6.29m	5.99m	8.07m	–	2.33m
2	0.86m	2.97m	3.86m	5.48m	6.90m	6.19m	5.89m	7.92m	–	2.21m
1	0.60m	2.89m	3.75m	5.38m	6.70m	6.09m	5.79m	7.77m	9.6	2.13m

7. Jumping Skills

Obviously to produce the real thing, work needs to be done off full approaches – but whilst this is desirable, it is not possible to reproduce many successive jumps at the required high level. It therefore becomes important that the jumper has a suitable short approach from which the skills can be expressed. The novice may be able to produce these off 7 strides, whereas the experienced jumper may require 11 strides or so.

In the case of short approach work, it is essential that the coach keeps a keen eye on technique to ensure that poor running ability or poor rhythm are not allowed to develop in the session. Body lean is a common fault here, when the athlete is trying to develop speed, sticking the bottom out; another is low running (lack of full leg extension). These can all be seen, so it requires keen coaching to be operating for such sessions.

The Jumps Decathlon table shown on pages 39-39 is an invaluable method of developing jumping skills and awareness. But it can equally be abused by overuse to become the end product, rather than one of the means to develop certain skills or specific strengths. Some of the activities can be used in greater numbers to provide heavier loadings for the mature athlete. Multiple skip drills over distances of 150m are used by some experienced athletes.

The opportunity should be taken for the coach to observe and monitor these activities. Such things as good use of the arms and a suitable head position are all important aspects which can be easily seen whilst the athlete competes. The Jumps Decathlon provides very useful motivation during the winter preparation period.

Figure 33

Mark Forsyth competing for Great Britain. Photograph by Gray Mortimore/Allsport

Training Schedules

This is where all coaches have their own ideas. It is where the individual planning as indicated in earlier chapters comes into its own. The pre-winter discussions, planning, replanning and revising are all important aspects of a coach's and an athlete's development.

Where there are complete beginners, it is important to realise that the long jumping part of preparation will need to fit in with other events and other training, not only during one session, but perhaps throughout the whole preparation period for one year. Keeping this in mind, it has been assumed that the very basics of the event have been taught and practised.

Beginners

1. Normal preparation of jogging and mobility routine done with all the group.
2. Specific long jump mobility exercises which need to cover the lower back, hip and hamstring.
3. 6-8 short approach jumps, 7-9 strides on runway. Choose one particular aspect of the approach to emphasise, eg running rhythm, head position. Work on one point at a time in the approach plus good active take-off.
4. 3 or 4 approach runs off a slightly longer approach, checking if running technique deteriorates as the board approaches, etc.
5. Series of acceleration runs to simulate approach run work, 4-6 x 40m.

The athletes may then be moving to another event, or joining another group to cover endurance aspects of training. The long jump phase of the training session needs quality, not quantity, to (1) produce good technical opportunity, (2) maintain interest, (3) show improvement.

Young Club Athletes

These are athletes who attend sessions on two or three occasions a week throughout the winter and want to make long jump one of their events.

This particular specialist training can perhaps be fitted in twice every two or three weeks in the winter.

A
1. Warm up – jogging.
2. Mobility exercises followed by specific long jump stretching.
3. Long jump preparation, choosing a particular aspect of the approach or take-off which you feel needs emphasis. This could be fast foot strike – for this skip drills are a very relevant practice; 12-15 contacts x 4-8 – emphasising good body position and fast feet.
4. Series of short approach jumps, 8-10. Again, choose a point to work on. Do not flit from one to another; it will only confuse the young athletes.
5. 140-130-120-100m sprints; walk back recovery.
6. Warm down.

B
1. Warm up.
2. Mobility, general and specific.
3. Sprint drills – choose those very relevant to long jump.
4. Acceleration runs 20 build up – 20 fast – 20 controlled x 4-6.
5. Big stride drill, plus some easy hops and jumps.
6. Warm down.

Summer
Obviously the sessions in the summer need to be different, or certainly show development on the theme the coach has chosen for the winter.

A

1+2 as established routine.

3.   Skip drills with emphasis on speed contact. 8-10 contacts x 2-4.

4.   Jumping 3/4 jumps off a 7/9 stride approach; 3/4 off an 11/13 strides; then, if competitions allow, 2/3 jumps off a full approach. Again choose to emphasise a particular individual coaching point. Allow ample recovery between efforts, and also before moving on to a stride session 80-60-40-20m with a walk back.

5.   Warm down.

B

1+2 as usual.

3.   Sprint drills.

4.   Rhythm runs on the runway x 3/4.

5.   Accuracy runs x 3/4. Remember the point made earlier: a take-off is essential on these efforts.

6.   Bounding/rhythm jumps. Not a large number of contacts; more to provide a positive attitude. Not on a Thursday before a Saturday competition. Give time to recover.

7.   Warm down.

Senior/Mature Club Athletes

Here we can assume the athletes are training 4/5 times per week.

Winter *M*

A

1.   Warm up.

2.   Mobility – general and specific.

3.   Strength training. Choose 6-8 exercises, which can include weight training and general fitness work. Alternate the exercises to ensure a fully beneficial workout is carried out. Activities could include:

Front squats
Power cleans
Hang snatch
Squat jumps with bar
Step-ups
Sprint arms – with dumbbells
Various types of squats

Sit-ups
Back raises
Side raises

4.   Relaxed stride session with walk back over 60m x 4-8. This will help clear localised lactic build up, which in turn may help to prevent injuries.

5.   Warm down.

B *T*

1.   Warm up.

2.   Mobility.

3.   Strides – walk back.

4.   Sprint drills.

5.   180-160-140-120-100m with a suitable recovery particular to each athlete.

6.   Reasonable recovery.

7.   Jumps circuit training.

8.   Warm down.

C *W*

A variation of session A, followed by 10/15 minutes Fartlek which should include 8-12 efforts varying in time from 10 sec to 25 seconds.

D *Th*

1.   Warm up.

2.   Mobility.

3.   Rhythm runs over 60m x 4/6; walk back.

4.   Short approach runs on runway.

5.   Bounding session – remember to control the contacts.

6.   Warm down.

E *FRI*

1.   Warm up.

2.   Mobility.

3.   Hill running session – 60-80m x 4-6 x 2/3; walk back recovery. Subject to suitable variation as ability improves.

4.   General fitness session.

5.   Warm down.

Summer

Again 4/5 times each week plus competition. Here it is important to arrange sessions to ensure that the competition does not follow a very hard training session. Perhaps it should follow a rest day. It becomes very individual at this stage, with all athletes having personal feelings on whether to rest the day before competition or do some activity.

A
1. Warm up.
2. Mobilise.
3. Sprint drills.
4. 4-6 rhythm runs on runway.
5. Short approach jumps for technique.
6. Warm down.

B
1. Warm up.
2. Mobilise.
3. Strides.
4. Weight training, perhaps emphasising two or three specialist exercises – Front squats/Power cleans/Squat jumps. The % of weight should be perhaps 60-70% of winter maximums. Alternate the lifting with explosive free jumps, two footed and one footed.
5. 6 x 60m strides; walk back.
6. Warm down.

C
1. Warm up.
2. Mobilise.
3. Strides; walk back.
4. Fitness session.
5. 150-130-110-90-70m; walk back recovery.
6. Warm down.

D
1. Warm up.
2. Mobilise.
3. Strides; walk back.
4. Further session of rhythm and accuracy runs on runway.
5. Series of short approach technical jumps.
6. Sprint running 60-50-40-30-20m.
   Quality runs; walk back, ample recovery.
7. Warm down.

Note:
All these schedules are merely starting points for individual planning. They are not in any particular order, nor do they include many support activities which athletes and coaches like to include in programmes. The training programme content must always reflect the actual fitness level of the athlete, not the theoretical level. Fit everything to your situation.

A Basic Guide to Long Jumpers' Problems

What you may see	*What you hope to see*
1. Inconsistent run up	Eventually a more constant stride length.
2. Too long a run up, slowing at take off	Short quick run up with speed through to take-off
3. Lack of height	Height in all jumps
4. Legs remain relatively straight before jump	Bending of knees, active take-off
5. Lack of effort at take-off (tired)	Explosive action at take-off
6. Arms staying in a low position	Arms move upwards at take-off
7. Head forward and looking down	Looking ahead
8. Flat footed landings with straight legs	Knees bending as heels contact the sand
And many more problems	Many more answers

APPENDIX III

Basic Fitness Circuit

These could be carried out: 20 sec exercises. 10 sec recovery – 1 minute between sets 2/3/4 x etc.

1.

2.

3. Fitness with Jumping Activities

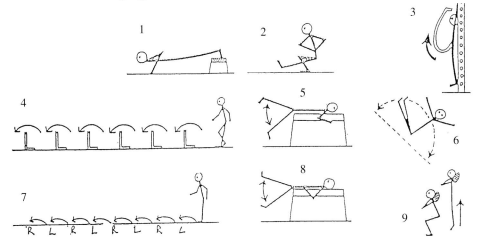

4. All Round General Fitness

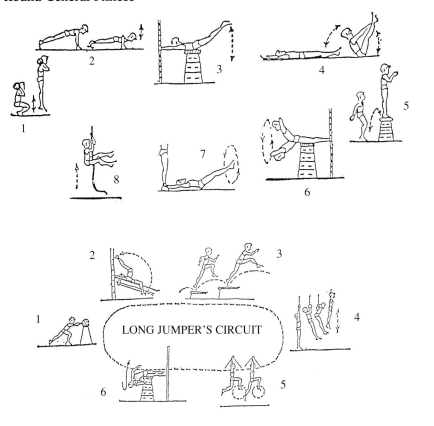

LONG JUMPER'S CIRCUIT

Drills and practices for advanced athletes

Note that the right foot is the black one in the practices.

APPENDIX V

Testing Your Athletes

This aspect is an important part of the yearly programme. It can provide motivation as well as relevant facts on the effectiveness of the training. It must always be remembered that these tests are guides, not actual training. They need to be reliable and objective to provide a valid result. Remember, however, that the most valid test is the competition result.

Tests can cover most aspects of preparation:

Speed, strength, endurance, actual jumping ability, flexibility.

The important feature of testing certain aspects of training is to be consistent in your testing – same venue, same conditions, same timing system etc – otherwise the results will be of no value to compare later.

Speed
Standing starts of 30-50m.
Block starts over 30-60m.
Rolling starts – acceleration phase timed between two fixed timers etc.

Endurance
600-1000m is an endurance situation for most long jump orientated athletes. Treadmill testing, oxygen uptake testing can all be done at specialist centres today.

Strength
The use of any lift in weight training exercises – 100%, 6 lifts, 10 reps etc. Within many fitness centres now it is possible to have any particular muscle group accurately tested by qualified personnel.

Mobility
Again an area which can be tested simply, but likewise done in many sophisticated ways by specialists today.

Jumping ability
This can be done by using the Jumps Decathlon scoring tables already shown. Choose any exercise as your guide. The stretch jump exercise (Sargent jump) can frequently be used today as most leisure centres have suitable boards.

All testing can be useful, especially if it is carried out regularly 3/4 times a year. But remember it is a guide, a support service to your planning of a suitable programme, one suitable for a beginner or a mature athlete.

APPENDIX VI

Progressive Lists of Records

World Records from 1901
Men

7.61 metres	Peter O'Connor	GBR	05/08/1901
7.69 metres	Edward Gourdin	USA	23/07/1921
7.76 metres	Robert LeGendre	USA	07/07/1924
7.89 metres	William de Hart Hubbard	USA	13/06/1925
7.90 metres	Edward Hamm	USA	07/07/1928
7.93 metres	Sylvio Cator	HAITI	09/09/1928
7.98 metres	Chuhei Nambu	JAP	27/10/1931
8.13 metres	Jesse Owens	USA	25/05/1935
8.21 metres	Ralph Boston	USA	12/08/1960
8.24 metres	Ralph Boston	USA	27/05/1961
8.28 metres	Ralph Boston	USA	16/07/1961
8.31 metres	Igor Ter-Ovanesyan	URS	10/06/1962
8.31 metres	Ralph Boston	USA	15/08/1964
8.34 metres	Ralph Boston	USA	12/09/1964
8.35 metres	Ralph Boston	USA	12/05/1965
8.35metres	Igor Ter-Ovanesyan	URS	19/10/1967
8.90 metres	Bob Beamon	USA	18/10/1968
8.95 metres	Mike Powell	USA	30/08/1991

World Records from 1928
Women

5.98 metres	Kinue Hitomi	JAP	20/05/1928
6.12 metres	Christel Schulz	FRG	30/07/1939
6.25 metres	Fanny Blankers-Koen	HOL	19/09/1943
6.28 metres	Yvette Williams	NZL	20/02/1954
6.28 metres	Galina Vinogradova	URS	11/09/1955
6.31 metres	Galina Vinogradova	URS	18/11/1955
6.35 metres	Elzbieta Kresinska	POL	20/08/1956
6.35 metres	Elzbieta Kresinska	POL	27/11/1956
6.40 metres	Hildrun Klaus	GDR	07/08/1960
6.42 metres	Hildrun Klaus	GDR	23/06/1961
6.48 metres	Tatyana Shchelkanova	URS	16/07/1961
6.53 metres	Tatyana Shchelkanova	URS	10/06/1962
6.70 metres	Tatyana Shchelkanova	URS	04/07/1964
6.76 metres	Mary Rand	GBR	14/10/1964
6.82 metres	Viorica Viscopoleanu	ROM	14/10/1968
6.84 metres	Heide Rosendahl	FRG	03/09/1970

6.92 metres	Angela Voigt	GDR	09/05/1976
6.99 metres	Sigrun Siegl	GDR	19/05/1976
7.07 metres	Vilma Bardauskiene	URS	18/08/1978
7.09 metres	Vilma Bardauskiene	URS	29/08/1978
7.15 metres	Anisoara Cusmir	ROM	01/08/1982
7.20 metres	Vali Ionescu	ROM	01/08/1982
7.21 metres	Anisoara Cusmir	ROM	15/05/1983
7.27 metres	Anisoara Cusmir	ROM	04/06/1983
7.43 metres	Anisoara Cusmir	ROM	04/06/1983
7.44 metres	Heike Drechsler	GDR	22/09/1985
7.45 metres	Heike Drechsler	GDR	21/06/1986
7.45 metres	Heike Drechsler	GDR	03/07/1986
7.52 metres	Galina Chistyakaova	URS	11/06/1988

Brtitish Records from 1862
Men

6.37 metres	C.F. Buller	?/03/1862
6.39 metres	A.C. Tosswill	21/03/1868
6.50 metres	A.C. Tosswill	21/03/1868
6.75 metres	A.C. Tosswill	27/02/1869
6.85 metres	Jenner Davies	25/03/1872
6.97 metres	Jenner Davies	27/03/1874
7.05 metres	John Lane (Ireland)	07/06/1874
7.06 metres	Patrick Davin (Ireland)	30/08/1883
7.06 metres	Patrick Davin (Ireland)	27/09/1883
7.08 metres	John Purcell (Ireland)	26/08/1886
7.08 metres	John Purcell (Ireland)	26/08/1886
7.14 metres	Charles Fry	08/04/1892
7.17 metres	Charles Fry	04/03/1893
7.21 metres	J.J. Mooney (Ireland)	05/09/1894
7.24 metres	William Newburn (Ireland)	18/06/1898
7.33 metres	William Newburn (Ireland)	16/07/1898
7.51 metres	Peter O'Connor (Ireland)	29/08/1900
7.54 metres	Peter O'Connor (Ireland)	27/05/1901
7.60 metres	Peter O'Connor (Ireland)	15/07/1901
7.61 metres	Peter O'Connor (Ireland)	28/07/1901
7.61 metres	Peter O'Connor (Ireland)	05/08/1901
7.63 metres	John Howell	14/08/1960
7.72 metres	Lynn Davies	26/11/1962
7.72 metres	John Morbey	23/08/1963
7.72 metres	John Morbey	08/05/1964
8.01 metres	Lynn Davies	16/05/1964
8.02 metres	Lynn Davies	25/07/1964

8.07 metres	Lynn Davies	18/11/1964
8.13 metres	Lynn Davies	06/04/1966
8.18 metres	Lynn Davies	09/04/1966
8.23 metres	Lynn Davies	30/06/1968

Women

5.05 metres	Mary Lines	20/08/1922
5.17 metres	Mary Lines	28/06/1924
5.24 metres	Phyllis Green	06/06/1925
5.48 metres	Muriel Gunn	02/08/1926
5.60 metres	Muriel Gunn	09/07/1927
5.68 metres	Muriel Gunn	14/07/1928
5.78 metres	Muriel Gunn	13/07/1929
5.80 metres	Muriel Gunn	21/06/1930
5.85 metres	Muriel Gunn	26/07/1930
5.92 metres	Shirley Cawley	23/07/1952
6.10 metres	Jean Desforges	30/08/1953
6.14 metres	Sheila Hoskin	05/05/1956
6.20 metres	Mary Rand	01/08/1959
6.27 metres	Mary Rand	14/05/1960
6.33 metres	Mary Rand	31/08/1960
6.35 metres	Mary Rand	13/07/1963
6.44 metres	Mary Rand	05/08/1963
6.58 metres	Mary Rand	04/07/1964
6.76 metres	Mary Rand	14/10/1964
6.90 metres	Beverley Kinch	14/08/1983

HD9

HD8

HD18

HD17

LARRY MYRICKS
(U.S.A.)

LM1

LM2

LM9

LM10

HD3

HD2

HD1

HEIKE DRECHSLER
(Germany)

HD12

HD11

HD10

LM6

LM7

LM8

LM14

LM15

LM16

HD6 HD5 HD4

HD15 HD14 HD13

LM4 LM5

LM12 LM13